CW01374202

Here I am on my First Holy Communion Day

This book belongs to

A gift on My First Communion on this date

In this Church

From

My First Holy Communion Mass Programme or Invitation

Jesus Speaks to Me

ON MY FIRST HOLY
COMMUNION

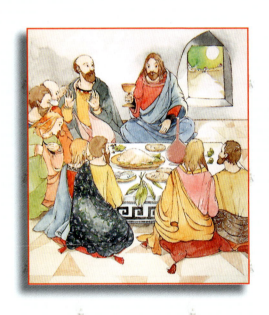

BY ANGELA M. BURRIN

ILLUSTRATED BY MARIA CRISTINA LO CASCIO

Creation

"God saw everything he had made, and it was very good."

Genesis 1:31

I am Jesus. And I want to say, "Happy First Holy Communion Day!"

I am so joyful that you have received me for the first time in the Eucharist. What a great day for both of us. It is the beginning of our special friendship.

Let me tell you about myself. Long, long before the creation of the world—even before the dinosaurs—I was in heaven with my Father and the Holy Spirit. We three, the Holy Trinity, are a family of love.

But we didn't want to keep our love to ourselves. We wanted to share it. My Father wanted children. So my Father created an awesome world for his children to live in. Try to name something he created that begins with each letter of the alphabet, from A to Z.

My Father planned for you to be part of his family. He loves you. Your heavenly "Daddy" knew your parents, your birthday, where you would live, and even the date of your First Holy Communion. You are his special child.

I'm so happy you are part of our family of love.

"Jesus, thank you for my First Holy Communion Day."

Adam and Eve

"God created people in his own image."
Genesis 1:27

Adam and Eve were the first people in our family of love. They lived in the beautiful Garden of Eden. My Father let them name all the animals. That must have been fun! And every evening, they walked and talked with him—just the way I want to talk with you each day, and especially after you receive Communion at Mass.

Now Adam and Eve could eat whatever they liked in the Garden—except for one thing. My Father told them not to eat the fruit of one tree in the middle of the Garden. Satan wanted to tempt them to disobey my Father, so he said to them, "That fruit is very good." Adam and Eve made a wrong choice; they ate the fruit.

Adam and Eve had disobeyed their heavenly Father. They knew they had done wrong. They had to leave the Garden of Eden. Their sin separated them and all their descendants from our family of love. But my Father promised, "I will send my only Son. He will bring my children back into our family of love."

"Jesus, I love you. I'm happy I can talk to you after Communion and at other times during my day."

The Call of Abraham

"YOUR CHILDREN WILL BE AS MANY AS THE STARS IN HEAVEN."
GENESIS 15:5

Remember, my Father never stopped loving Adam and Eve and their descendants. He had a plan to save them and bring them back to him.

One day, my Father called out to a man named Abram, saying, "Leave your home. I promise to show you where to go." Abram trusted and obeyed. With his wife, Sara, and their relatives, servants, and animals, they began a

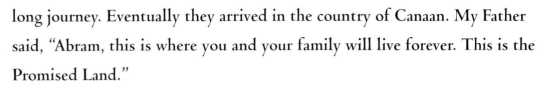

long journey. Eventually they arrived in the country of Canaan. My Father said, "Abram, this is where you and your family will live forever. This is the Promised Land."

Abram then had a few more surprises. My Father said, "You will be the father of my special family. Your children will be as many as the stars in heaven. And your new name is Abraham."

Did you know that I'm one of Abraham's descendants? And so are you! I'm your brother! When you receive the Eucharist, think of me as your big brother. You can trust me and tell me anything. Also, ask me to bless the people you love. I will always listen to you.

"Jesus, my brother, I trust you."

The Passover

"Look, the Lamb of God!"
John 1:29

My Father's special family had many adventures. Let's fast forward. They are now called Israelites. They live in Egypt, and Moses is their leader.

The Israelites were the slaves of Pharaoh, the ruler of Egypt. But my Father wanted to free them. He sent Moses to tell Pharaoh, "Let my people go." But when Pharaoh refused, my Father sent terrible plagues.

So my Father told Moses, "Tomorrow you will escape. Prepare and eat a meal of roasted lamb, bitter herbs, and unleavened bread. And put the blood of the lamb over your doors for protection from the angel of death." That night all the firstborn of the Egyptians died. But the Israelites were kept safe.

The Israelites called their last meal in Egypt *Passover* because the angel of death had passed over them. Then Moses led his people out of Egypt by parting the Red Sea with his walking stick. Now they had passed from slavery to freedom.

At Mass the priest holds up the host, saying, "This is the Lamb of God." I am my Father's Passover Lamb. At Communion you can also receive the wine. This is my Precious Blood. Just as the blood of the lamb protected the Israelites, so my Blood will protect you.

"Jesus, thank you for your precious Blood!"

Manna in the Desert

"I AM THE BREAD OF HEAVEN."
JOHN 6:51

What kind of foods do you like to eat? When I was growing up, children loved raisin cakes and corn popped in the sun.

Food is very important. When people don't have enough to eat, they get tired and weak. That's what happened to the Israelites after they escaped from Pharaoh.

The journey through the desert back to Canaan was very long. Food was hard to find. Everyone was hungry. Some complained to Moses, "In Egypt we had lots to eat." My Father heard them and told Moses, "Tomorrow, I will rain down bread from heaven!"

When the Israelites woke up, the ground was covered with white flakes! They called it manna—bread from heaven. Every morning, the men collected enough manna for their families. Now they had strength for their journey.

Didn't my Father take good care of his family? And he does the same for you. He's given you *me* in the Eucharist. I am your spiritual food! After Communion, tell me what you might need. Perhaps it's help with your schoolwork, or with being obedient, honest, forgiving, or kind. I will help you to be a strong Christian.

"JESUS, I NEED YOUR HELP RIGHT NOW WITH . . . "
(TELL JESUS WHAT IT IS).

The Birth of Jesus

"A Saviour has been born."
LUKE 2:11

Do you like Christmas? It's all about my birth. I'm the Saviour my Father promised would bring the descendants of Adam and Eve back into our family of love.

My Father chose a young Israelite teenager called Mary to bring about his promise. He sent the angel Gabriel to Mary to ask her to become my mother. Mary said, "Yes!" Joseph agreed to marry Mary and care for her and her baby.

I was born in Bethlehem. A kind innkeeper let Mary and Joseph use his stable. After my birth, Mary placed me on straw in a manger. The animals' breath kept me warm. And that night, something wonderful happened. Thousands of angels sang, "Glory to God!" Shepherds in the nearby fields saw and heard the angels. They came to visit me. Later, I had a visit from three wise men. They brought me precious gifts.

You can visit me too. I'm always present in the Eucharist in the tabernacle at your church. Before Mass begins, kneel down and say, "Jesus, I love you. Thank you for leaving heaven and becoming human like me."

"Jesus, I want to be like Mary our Mother,
who was humble and obedient."

Jesus Feeds the Five Thousand

"THEY ALL HAD ENOUGH TO EAT."
LUKE 9:17

Do you like hearing about miracles? I'll tell you one that I did by the power of the Holy Spirit!

On a hot day, lots of adults and children followed me up a hillside. Some had travelled a long way. I told them that my Father loved them, just like I tell you. I also asked them to forgive one another. The disciples, my special friends, were with me. Just as the sun was setting, they said, "Jesus, the people are hungry. Send them home." Then one said, "There's a boy here with five barley loaves and two fish. But that's not enough to feed everyone."

After the people sat down, I took the loaves and fishes and blessed them. The disciples gave them to the crowd. Everyone had enough to eat. The leftovers filled twelve baskets. I fed over five thousand people that day.

Isn't that an awesome miracle? And what a memory those people had of my care for them. But I've given you more than a memory. I, Jesus, give you myself in the Eucharist. That's the closest we'll be until you're with me in heaven!

"JESUS, PLEASE FEED THE HUNGRY PEOPLE OF THE WORLD TODAY."

Jesus Blesses the Children

"LET THE LITTLE CHILDREN COME TO ME."
LUKE 18:16

I love children. And that includes you. I think about you all the time.

And I loved being with children when I lived on earth. One day some parents wanted to bring their children to me for a blessing. But because I was teaching the people stories about my Father's heavenly kingdom, my disciples stopped them. "Jesus is busy. Take your children away," they said.

"No, let the children come to me," I said. "They too are part of my Father's special family." The children came running. Several girls gave me flowers. Some boys climbed on my back. A toddler jumped on my lap and stroked my beard. If you had been there, what would you have done and said to me?

Before the children left, I blessed them. And as they waved goodbye, many shouted out, "Jesus, you're my best friend."

I've also given you many blessings. After receiving me in the Eucharist, close your eyes, imagine I am there with you, and thank me for some of them—your parents, your friends, the beautiful world I created, and lots more!

"JESUS, THANK YOU FOR BEING MY FRIEND.
HELP ME TO BE A GOOD FRIEND TO OTHERS."

The Last Supper

"DO THIS IN MEMORY OF ME." *LUKE 22:19*

"Dinner's ready!" I always stopped what I was doing when I heard my mother call that out. Mary, Joseph, and I loved eating our meals together.

The evening before I died on the cross, I ate a Passover meal with my twelve disciples in an upper room in Jerusalem. We remembered and celebrated how Moses led my Father's special family out of slavery in Egypt into the Promised Land.

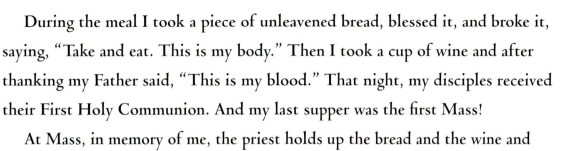

During the meal I took a piece of unleavened bread, blessed it, and broke it, saying, "Take and eat. This is my body." Then I took a cup of wine and after thanking my Father said, "This is my blood." That night, my disciples received their First Holy Communion. And my last supper was the first Mass!

At Mass, in memory of me, the priest holds up the bread and the wine and repeats my words. And by the power of the Holy Spirit, the bread and wine become my body and blood. This is called the Consecration. During this time, look, listen, and say in your heart, "Jesus, I believe you are really present in the Eucharist."

"Jesus, thank you for the Eucharist."

Jesus Dies on the Cross

"Forgive us our sins."
Luke 11:4

As the Saviour of the world, I knew my Father's plan was for me to die on a cross.

So after the Last Supper, I took my disciples to the Garden of Gethsemane. They fell asleep, but I prayed to my Father for strength to accept what he wanted me to do.

Suddenly, Roman soldiers carrying torches came and arrested me. Judas, one of my friends, had told them where I was.

The next day, the soldiers put a crown of thorns on my head. They made me carry a heavy cross up the Hill of Calvary. I fell three times. On the way I met my mother. After hanging on the cross for six hours, I died.

I took on myself all the sins of the world. Now my Father's children are forgiven and can again be part of our family of love. During Mass, think about what happened on Holy Thursday and Good Friday. After receiving Communion, thank me for dying on the cross for your sins. And remember: no sin is too big to be forgiven.

"Jesus, thank you for being the Saviour of the world."

The Resurrection of Jesus

"I AM WITH YOU ALWAYS."
MATTHEW 28:20

I'm alive. I've risen from the dead!

On Sunday, the first day of the Jewish week, the women went to the tomb and found it empty. I surprised everyone!

After my resurrection, I met up with my disciples in homes, on roads, and as they fished on the Sea of Galilee. We spent forty happy days together.

I explained to them that although I would be leaving them soon, I would always be with them. I asked them to tell everyone about me—about my life, death, and resurrection. I promised to send my Holy Spirit to help them.

I took my disciples to the Mount of Olivet. After blessing them I ascended to heaven, where I am now with my Father and the Holy Spirit in our family of love.

Just like my disciples, you cannot see me. But I am always with you. In the morning say, "Good Morning, Jesus." During the day, whether you're happy or worried, say, "Jesus, you're with me." And before going to sleep, listen to me say, "I love you!"

"JESUS, I'M SO HAPPY YOU ARE ALWAYS CLOSE TO ME,
ESPECIALLY IN THE EUCHARIST."

Pentecost,
the Birthday of the Church

"THEY WERE ALL FILLED WITH THE HOLY SPIRIT."
ACTS 2:4

I kept my promise!

After I was lifted up into heaven, my disciples and others went back to the upper room in Jerusalem, locked the doors, and prayed. On the tenth day, they heard a loud noise. It sounded like a strong wind. Then they saw fire flames over each others' heads. They shouted, "It's the Holy Spirit!"

That day, Pentecost, was the beginning of my Church. It is the Church's birthday!

Now the Holy Spirit did amazing things in the disciples' hearts. They were no longer afraid. They ran out into the streets and told everyone, "Jesus is alive. He wants you to be with him forever in heaven."

Many people wanted to know more about me. So they joined the disciples. They celebrated Mass in their homes. Peter became the head of the Church.

You became a member of our family, the Church, when you received the Sacrament of Baptism.

And now you have made your First Holy Communion!

My last words to you are, "I love you. And please keep loving me in the Eucharist."

"JESUS, I LOVE YOU. THANK YOU FOR YOUR HOLY SPIRIT!"

The Sign of the Cross

In the name of the Father

and of the Son

and of the Holy Spirit.

Amen.

The Glory Be

Glory be to the Father,

and to the Son, and

to the Holy Spirit.

As it was in the beginning,

is now, and ever shall be,

world without end.

Amen.

The Our Father

Our Father, who art in heaven,

hallowed be your name;

your kingdom come;

your will be done

on earth as it is in heaven.

Give us this day our daily bread;

and forgive us our trespasses

as we forgive those

who trespass against us;

and lead us not into temptation,

but deliver us from evil.

Amen.

The Hail Mary

Hail Mary, full of grace,

the Lord is with you.

Blessed are you among women,

and blessed is the fruit of your womb, Jesus.

Holy Mary, Mother of God,

pray for us sinners,

now and at the hour of our death.

Amen.

Act of Contrition

My God, I am sorry for my sins with all my heart.

In choosing to do wrong and failing to do good,

I have sinned against you whom I should love above

all things.

I firmly intend with your help,

to do penance, to sin no more,

and to avoid whatever leads me to sin. Amen.

The Apostles' Creed

I believe in God, the Father almighty,

creator of heaven and earth.

I believe in Jesus Christ, his only Son, our Lord.

He was conceived by the power of the Holy Spirit

and born of the Virgin Mary.

He suffered under Pontius Pilate,

was crucified, died, and was buried.

He descended to the dead.

On the third day he rose again.

He ascended into heaven,

and is seated at the right hand of the Father.

He will come again to judge the living and the dead.

I believe in the Holy Spirit,

the holy catholic Church,

the communion of saints,

the forgiveness of sins,

the resurrection of the body,

and the life everlasting.

Amen.

The Gloria

Glory to God in the highest,
and peace to his people on earth.

Lord God, heavenly King,
almighty God and Father,
we worship you, we give you thanks,
we praise you for your glory.

Lord Jesus Christ, only Son of the Father,
Lord God, Lamb of God,
you take away the sin of the world:
have mercy on us;
you are seated at the right hand of the Father:
receive our prayer.

For you alone are the Holy One,
you alone are the Lord,
you alone are the Most High,
Jesus Christ,
with the Holy Spirit,
in the glory of God the Father. Amen.

Prayer to My Guardian Angel

Angel of God, my guardian dear,

to whom God's love commits me here,

every day (night)

be at my side,

to light and guard,

to rule and guide. Amen.

These people came to my First Holy Communion

This is what I want to especially remember about my First Holy Communion

Photos of my First Holy Communion

Photos of my First Holy Communion

Photos of *My First Holy Communion*

Photos of My First Holy Communion

Published in the UK by Redemptorist Publications
Alphonsus House, Chawton, Hampshire, GU34 3HQ
Telephone 01420 88222 Fax 01420 88805
rp@rpbooks.co.uk www.rpbooks.co.uk

ISBN 978-0-85231-356-5

First edition 2008

Copyright © 2008 Anno Domini Publishing
Book House, Orchard Mews, 18 High Street, Tring, Herts HP23 5AH England
www.ad-publishing.com
Text copyright © 2008 Angela M. Burrin
Illustrations copyright © 2008 Maria Cristina lo Cascio

Publishing Director: Annette Reynolds
Editor: Nicola Bull
Art Director: Gerald Rogers
Pre-production: Krystyna Kowalska Hewitt
Production: John Laister

Printed and bound in Dubai